ROSS on WILDE:
"To talk with him was to be translated to an enchanted island or to the palaces of the *Fata Morgana*. You could not tell what flowers were at your feet or what fantastic architecture was silhouetted against the purple atmosphere of his conversation."

LEVERSON on WILDE:
"By the time Art-coal-scuttles had reached Balham, people who, when first fired by the fervid words of the young Oscar, had thrown their mahogany into the streets, were looking out for red-and-white-ivory chessmen, wax-flowers under glass, little horse-hair sofas and 'lustres,' desiring to have one perfect middle-Victorian room."

"With his extraordinary high spirits and love of fun, he appealed to the lower classes; his higher gifts enchanted the artistic and such of the great world as wanted to amuse themselves; and with the sincere artist he was most himself. But the lower middle-class never liked him, always distrusted him and disliked his success."

WILDE on WILDE:
"Nothing pains me except stupidity."

"Treachery is inseparable from faith; I often betray myself with a kiss."

"Am so pleased, my dear Sphinx. No other voice but yours is musical enough to echo my music. I rely on you to misrepresent me."

LETTERS TO THE SPHINX

WALMER BELLES-LETTRES

1. Letters to a Friend *Winifred Holtby*
2. The Letters of Lord Byron
3. Letters to the Sphinx *Oscar Wilde*

LETTERS TO THE SPHINX

from

OSCAR WILDE

with

REMINISCENCES OF THE AUTHOR

by

ADA LEVERSON

and a note of explanation by

ROBERT ROSS

ADELAIDE
MICHAEL WALMER
2015

Letters to the Sphinx first published (in a limited edition of 275 copies) 1930

This edition published 2015

by

Michael Walmer
49 Second Street
Gawler South
South Australia 5118

ISBN 978-0-9944306-0-1 paperback
ISBN 978-0-9944306-1-8 ebook

ERRATA
This edition has been prepared utilizing a previous edition; thus errors have been reproduced. On page 59, the date of the second letter should read 2.5.1895

FOR
RAYMOND

I wish to thank the Literary Executor of the estate of the late Oscar Wilde for very kindly giving me permission to publish the Letters to the Sphinx.

ADA LEVERSON

Washington Hotel,
    Curzon Street,
        Mayfair
February 10, 1930

Contents

A Note of Explanation, by Robert Ross	13
Reminiscences, by Ada Leverson	
1. The Importance of Being Oscar	19
2. The Last First Night	26
3. Afterwards	36
Letters to the Sphinx	50

A Note of Explanation*
By Robert Ross

THE writing of introductions to volumes which require none has become a serious impediment to the enjoyment of literature. In a translation, or in a work of abstruse learning, there is some excuse for the student gilding his researches with a preface from the pen of some acknowledged scholar; but this chaperonage of literature has been carried too far. Even the novels of the last century, obvious though they are, seem to require the pointed approval of the dowagers and doyens of letters before they can be reissued in the lapsed copyright editions!

The English classics have by this means floated many obscurities into the lagoons of *Who's Who*. Without the risk of being included in the salvage I have consented to write a few words of explanation, *not* introduction, to the following sheets.

* Some years ago, when it was intended to publish this book anonymously, Mr. Robert Ross kindly wrote this prefatory note. For various reasons publication has been delayed till now.

The author of this essay has, alas! elected to remain anonymous. And it is for this reason only that in my capacity of literary executor I have been asked to assure the friends and admirers of Oscar Wilde that the letters it contains *are* by *him;* a necessary precaution, owing to the spurious writings and the forged letters attributed to him. Let me add on my own account that the witty author of these impressions was a friend to whom Oscar Wilde owed, and gave, the homage of his intellect.

With the exception of Mr. Robert Sherard's (remarkable and interesting) life of Oscar Wilde, there is no (trustworthy) account in English of an author whose writings are only beginning to receive the appreciation in England accorded to them on the continent. While the only *personal* recollections published even there, to which any importance or belief can be attached, are those by Monsieur André Gide and Monsieur Ernest La Jeunesse—exact and truthful sketches from different points of view.

The publication of *De Profundis* revived the interest in a personality which, apart from sad associations, was unique in English literature. To many people that personality was a repellent one; to others such as the writer of this book it was peculiarly fascinating. It will always be difficult for us to convey to those who never knew him, or who, knowing him, disliked him, the extraordinary magnetism which he exercised at least on the needles, if not the silver churns, of life. As in the fable of a gold and silver shield every one received entirely different impressions according to the method of their approach and the accident of acquaintance. That I venture to differ from Mr. Sherard's view of our friend does not necessarily vitiate the truth of the picture he has given us. At all events, here is another picture equally true; and more in accord with my own visual memory.

To present Oscar Wilde completely, in the sense that Velasquez has presented Pope Innocent X, would require the comprehensive genius of Boswell, Purcell or Robert Browning. Neither the writer of this book, nor, I am sure, Mr. Sherard, nor myself, would lay claim to the necessary equipment. Perhaps it was some foreboding of our failings that made Oscar Wilde say 'every one should be his own Boswell' and that 'it is always Judas who writes the biography.' If Mr. Sherard's picture may be compared to sombre mezzotint, the author of this book has given, to me at all events, an exquisite pastel. I venture to hope that other friends and even enemies may endorse my opinion.

In writing of one whose egoism was superb it is impossible to be adequate without intruding the first person singular; only through the convention of Willoughby Patterne can we produce a negative of Oscar Wilde, and then the silver print always betrays over-exposure. It is impossible to echo even faintly that voice 'which conjured wonder out of emptiness.' He was indeed a conjurer. To talk with him was to be translated to an enchanted island or to the palaces of the *Fata Morgana*. You could not tell what flowers were at your feet or what fantastic architecture was silhouetted against the purple atmosphere of his conversation. What expert could date the pleasant furniture of his house of life? Who would not kneel in the chapels of that Rimmon? . . . But if Prospero is dead we value all the more the little memories of Miranda.

ROBERT ROSS

Nothing is better, I well think,
  Than love; the hidden well-water
Is not so delicate to drink:
  This was well seen of me and her.

                              SWINBURNE

Reminiscences

1. The Importance of Being Oscar

IN the middle 'nineties, wealth, though not so rare as it is now, was already becoming scarce; there was even some fear that money might entirely vanish from the earth; and when two capitalists were heard one June night singing in a wood near Esher, Oscar Wilde wrote to *The Times* about it immediately. Money was spoken of in undertones and in offices; it was desired and valued as it is now, although 'prices' were not a regular conventional subject of conversation.

There was more margin; margin in every sense was in demand, and I remember, looking at the poems of John Gray (then considered the incomparable poet of the age), when I saw the tiniest rivulet of text meandering through the very largest meadow of margin, I suggested to Oscar Wilde that he should go a step further than these minor poets; that he should publish a book *all* margin; full of beautiful unwritten thoughts, and have this blank volume bound in some Nile-green skin powdered with gilt nenuphars and smoothed with hard ivory, decorated with gold by Ricketts (if not Shannon) and printed on Japanese paper; each volume must be a collector's piece, a numbered one of a limited 'first' (and last) edition: 'very rare.'

He approved.

'It shall be dedicated to you, and the unwritten text illustrated by Aubrey Beardsley. There must be five hundred signed copies for particular friends, six for the general public, and one for America.'

At this time, 1894 to 1895, London bloomed out into a sudden flamboyance of taste and of expression. Art, poetry, beauty, dress and decoration became the fashion; such subjects were talked about by everyone, however little most of them knew about it. If the Sheik had not yet been invented, 'chic' was greatly desired; phrases such as 'quite wonderful,' 'simply perfect,' 'too lovely,' 'marvellous,' were the mode. Sentimental crises were discussed at great length and with leisurely enjoyment, with agonies of sympathy if unfortunate. The Overture to *Tannhäuser*, Daly's, the Gaiety, the Lyceum, *Mrs. Tanqueray* were subjects of enthusiasm quite un-English; it is often, in fact, a Briton rather than a foreigner who 'gushes' while the Frenchman understates. Where an Englishman might say of a well-cooked dish that it was 'quite perfect' or 'excellent,' the most a Frenchman would say would be 'Ça se mange.'

Where, in those days, was the strong silent man? Nowhere! Something weaker and more loquacious was required; and all these exuberant modes were certainly inaugurated by the poet-wit-dramatist Oscar Wilde; who loved, and made fashionable, rich brocades, rose-coloured tented-ceilings, yellow satin, 'a consolation for all the miseries of life'; jewels, and lavish flowers; in reaction from the severity and restraint of Morris and Ford Madox Brown and the other pre-Raphaelites, and also from the little Noah's-ark figures and the Noah's archaism of the forgotten aesthetic 'eighties. No more green and yellow! All was purple and gold. The hero of *Patience*, the subject of so many jests, had now a serious following. It was perhaps unfortunate that followers were allowed. Like all disciples, they had a way of being more Royalist than the King, remaining Royalist, indeed, after he had resigned, continuing to exploit a mode when its originator had long tired of it.

By the time Art-coal-scuttles had reached Balham, people who, when first fired by the fervid words of the young Oscar, had thrown their mahogany into the streets, were looking out for red-and-white-ivory chessmen, wax-flowers under glass, little horse-hair sofas and 'lustres,' desiring to have one perfect middle-Victorian room. The contrast in taste between the poet and his illustrator, Aubrey Beardsley, was very marked. Oscar loved purple and gold, Aubrey put everything down in black and white. And while every connoisseur declared the line of the young artist superb, there were others who deplored that he did not know where to draw it.

Life seemed very gay and easy then, and in superficial ways very much like the present time. The de Rezskes were singing, Lady de Grey encouraging music; Teddy Payne and Arthur Roberts amused us; and hadn't we Whistler, that great correspondent, always writing witty, insulting letters to people, publishing the letters at his own expense (and theirs), painting their portraits and tearing the pictures up in a rage, and always quarrelling until the public became quite confused in the grey mist as to which of the pictures was 'Battersea Bridge by Moonlight,' which 'Carlyle,' and which the 'Portrait of the Artist's Mother'?

The Apes-of-God (not long ago invented by Mr. Wyndham Lewis but then known as the Hounds of Heaven) felt it their duty, or made it their business, to 'burn with a hard gem-like flame' (Pater's orders), to 'shrink from no experience,' to 'seek sensations.' This emotional self-expression resulted in the fashion, in the 'nineties, of frequent letters. Long, witty, sentimental letters (sent by private hansom-cab, waiting-for-an-answer); passionate, long, reply-paid telegrams; while the call of the district-messenger-boy resounded in every home.

As Oscar Wilde himself once remarked, one can't go about abusing Heliogabalus, censuring Caesar Borgia, or scolding Nero. These figures have passed into the sphere of Art. So has our spectacular genius, Oscar Wilde. But the essential difference is that he was a man incapable of being either cruel or hard. The most soft-hearted, carelessly-generous and genial of men, his great fault was weakness, and, with all his brilliance, a fatal want of judgment. Yet he is like them because he has become a legend. He was always a legend. He always will be.

Quicker in repartee and conversation than in his writing, he constantly made use in his work, afterwards, of things he had improvised.

At a certain party I remember a serious young man, who, with others, was waiting his turn to speak to Oscar, asking him questions. The poet used several of these replies in his book *Intentions*.

"Will you very kindly tell me, Mr. Wilde, in your own words, your viewpoint of George Meredith?"

"George Meredith is a prose Browning, and so is Browning."

"Thank you. His style?"

"Chaos, illumined by flashes of lightning."

"And what do you think of Verlaine?"

"Verlaine is in the gutter, but he writes poetry on the pavement."

"And Rudyard Kipling?"

"Ah! He has found that great thing for success, a new background. All palm trees, salaams and whiskey-and-soda. His jaded Anglo-Indians show up on a superb background of vulgarity.

"He has seen some marvellous things through keyholes, has dropped more h's in his verse than any living man; *The Silver Man* is a masterpiece."

Another man here came up, interrupting and slapping the poet on the shoulder, exclaiming "Hullo, Oscar!"

Oscar looked up. He saw a stranger to him. He said, "I don't know you by sight, but your manner is familiar."

He told me that evening that a woman had come to him saying she had some screens sent from Japan, and asked him to advise her how to arrange them. "Don't arrange them. Let them occur."

A certain very kind and hospitable lady frequently invited Oscar to lunch and dine when he was at Dieppe after his troubles.

She was rather proud of her housekeeping economies, and mentioned that by buying a quantity at a time she paid very little for her wine. "How much do you think it costs?" she asked.

"I have no idea," said Oscar, tasting it.

"Only about ninepence a bottle!" she replied.

He drank a little more and put it down.

"Dreadful! It's curious; too bad, but wine-merchants always cheat women disgracefully!" murmured Oscar.

2. The Last First Night

On Valentine's day, the 14th February 1895, there was a snow-storm more severe than had been remembered in London for years. A black, bitter, threatening wind blew the drifting snow. On that dark sinister winter's night, when the first representation of *The Importance of being Earnest* was produced at the St. James's Theatre, it was with difficulty that one drove there at all, one had to go very slowly on account of the horses. Crowds of hansoms, broughams, carriages of all kinds blocked little King Street.

When at last we took refuge in the playhouse, how grateful was the contrast! Outside, a frost, inside, the very breath of success; perfumed atmosphere of gaiety, fashion and, apparently, everlasting popularity. The author of the play was fertile, inventive, brilliant; and with such encouragement how could one realise that the gaiety was not to last, that his life was to become dark, cold, sinister as the atmosphere outside? Perfumed; for had not the word gone forth from Oscar that the lily-of-the-valley was to be the flower of the evening, as a souvenir of an absent friend? Flowers meant much in those days, and nearly all the pretty women wore sprays of lilies against their large puffed sleeves, while rows and rows of young elegants had buttonholes of the delicate bloom of lilies-of-the-valley. Most of the smart young men held tall canes of ebony with ivory tops; they wore white gloves with rows of black stitching and very pointed shoes.

It was a distinguished audience, such as is rarely seen nowadays either at the Opera or even at a first night of a Russian Ballet. The street just outside was crowded, not only with the conveyances and the usual crowd of waiting people, but with other Wilde fanatics who appeared to regard the arrivals as part of the performance. Many of these shouted and cheered the best-known people, and the loudest cheers were for the author who was as well known as the Bank of England, as he got out of his carriage with his pretty wife, who afterwards joined friends when the author himself went behind the scenes.

What a rippling, glittering, chattering crowd was that! They were certain of some amusement, for if, by exception, they did not care for the play, was not Oscar himself sure to do something to amuse them? Would he perhaps walk on after the play smoking a cigarette, with a green carnation blooming savagely in his coat, and saying, in his slow way, with a slight smile (emphasizing certain words in the tradition of Swinburne), "The *play* is de*light*ful, I've enjoyed myself *so* much?" Or, as on another occasion, would he bow from a box and state in clear tones, heard all over the theatre, that Mr. Wilde was not in the house?

If he played to the Gallery, he got the Stalls.

There had been rumours for weeks that at Worthing Oscar was writing a farce, and how each day he wrote a part of it and each evening he read it to the Elect—his wife, children and a few friends. He himself said it was a delicate bubble of fancy, but in truth he cared little for any of his plays excepting only *Salome*.

Influenced as he had been at the time by Maeterlinck, Flaubert and Huysmans, yet *Salome* expressed *himself* in his innate love of the gorgeous and the bizarre. (He said it was indeed unique: for it was written by an Irishman in French and done into English by a young Scotch friend!)

But to return to his first night—to be the last—

For months before Lewis Waller had been

tender and manly as The Ideal Husband, Sir George Alexander superb as Lord Windermere and Beerbohm Tree had been witty and amusing in the favourite *A Woman of no Importance*. Oscar was, therefore, no novice. But he had not as yet written a farce.

Everyone was repeating his *mots*. Society at the moment was enthusiastic about that rarest of human creatures, a celebrity with good manners.

It is difficult now to convey in words the strange popularity, the craze there was at this moment for the subject of my essay. 'To meet Mr. Oscar Wilde' was put on the most exclusive of invitation cards, yet every omnibus conductor knew his latest jokes. If he were caviare to the general, he was gentleman's-relish to the particular. His greatest pleasure was to amuse the mob, to frighten the burgess and to fascinate the aristocrat.

With his extraordinary high spirits and love of fun, he appealed to the lower classes; his higher gifts enchanted the artistic and such of the great world as wanted to amuse themselves; and with the sincere artist he was most himself. But the lower middle-class never liked him, always distrusted him and disliked his success.

People as a rule do not object to a man deserving success, only to his getting it.

Whoever still lives who was present on that night will remember the continual ripple of laughter from the very first moment, the excitement, the strange almost hysterical joy with which was received this 'Trivial Comedy for Serious People.' In some ways it was almost childish fun.

For a long time Oscar had been criticised for his continual use of paradox and epigram, witty, apt and cynical as they were, and the fashion of that period. At times they were considered wearying in the other plays. But how much sense there was in them really.

'Men marry because they are tired, women because they are curious.'

'The cynic is a person who knows the price of everything and the value of nothing.'

'The good American goes to Paris when he dies. Where do the bad Americans go? They go to America.'

Oscar's style of wit lent itself only too dangerously to imitation, and for years we suffered from a plethora of half-witted epigrams and feeble paradoxes by the mimics of his manner.

He had resolved to have nothing of this formula of wit in the farce. There was even a rollicking pun in the title. He intended it should be all Pure Nonsense. There is not a *mot*, not a paradox in the play, but the unexpectedness of this method pleased all the more, and when the curtain went down after the first act (which seemed to be principally about cucumber-sandwiches) on the pathetic wail so well uttered by Allan Aynesworth, the childlike simplicity of the phrase 'But I haven't quite finished my tea!' was a triumph. Oscar had been right. When a friend said that the farce should be like a piece of mosaic, he answered "No; it must go like a pistol shot."

And how they laughed when dignified George Alexander arrived on the stage in the deepest mourning, for the imaginary funeral of the fictitious Bunbury, who had now become a nuisance to his creator and had to die! (Black-tipped cigarettes were even suggested, but Alexander drew the line there.)

After the next act Oscar came to my box in which were the Beardsleys, Mabel and Aubrey, and other friends.

Before I first met Oscar, several years earlier, I had been told that he was rather like a giant with the wings of a Brazilian butterfly and I was not disappointed. But I thought him far more like a Roman Emperor who should have lived at the Pavilion at Brighton with George IV.

He was on this evening at the zenith of his careless, genial career, beaming and filled with that *euphoria* that was curiously characteristic of him when he was not in actual grief or pain. He had a low wide brow, with straight heavy hair into which the iron had entered, thus giving him the look of a Roman bust. His face was a clear red-brown from a long stay by the sea. He had blue-grey eyes and a well-formed mouth curved by a perpetual smile, and often a laugh of sincere humorous enjoyment of life. He had a superb vitality, a short-sighted joy in living for the moment. All genius has its naïf side, and he, a spectacular genius, greater, perhaps, as an improvisor in conversation than as a writer, had this *naïveté* in excess. But I am not here intending to criticise either the work or the man; merely to give an impression of a period, and of one evening that has remained in my memory.

Oscar bore no trace, in 1895, of the pale

slender long-haired youth who had met Sarah Bernhardt on her first arrival in England, his arms full of Madonna lilies, and had introduced the 'New Helen,' the Jersey lily, the beautiful Mrs. Langtry, to Millais, who painted her portrait and introduced her to Royalty. Oscar had written reams of verse to her and was so much in love with her that he insisted on lying on her doorstep half the night, and in the snow, too, until Mr. Langtry, that legendary but yet, it seems, real figure, stumbled over him on returning from the club.

The poet was not now 'alone and palely loitering' like the victim of *La Belle Dame sans Merci*, 'the lady without a thank you' as the child translated it when the picture was hung in the Academy.

I can see Oscar now as he looked on the 14th February 1895. He was dressed with elaborate dandyism and a sort of florid sobriety. His coat had a black velvet collar. He held white gloves in his small pointed hands. On one finger he wore a large scarab ring. A green carnation, echo in colour of the ring, bloomed in his buttonhole, and a large bunch of seals on a black moiré ribbon watch-chain hung from his white waistcoat. This costume, which on another man might have appeared perilously like fancy dress, and on his imitators was nothing less, seemed to suit him perfectly; he seemed at ease and to have the look of the last gentleman in Europe.

"Don't sit on the same chair as Aubrey. It's not compromising," was his first remark. Aubrey Beardsley had a habit of folding up his long lank figure and perching on the arms of chairs. He had a quaint fund of rather sardonic humour, and was also a great dandy. He declared that he caught a bad cold by leaving the tassel off his cane.

"What a contrast the two are," Oscar continued, "Mabel a daisy, Aubrey the most monstrous of orchids."

The piece went splendidly, and we went after to supper at Willis's, a small restaurant then the fashion, famed for its cooking, its scarlet-leather seats and yellow candleshades, only a few doors from the theatre. And as we walked there in the mud and blinding sleet, what a shock, what a horrible contrast to the warmth, the perfume within! Oscar did not join us at supper as he usually did. Some dark forecast perhaps—some chill presentiment; or perhaps because of the strange behaviour of the Marquess of Queensberry, who had left at the box-office an extraordinary bouquet of carrots, cauliflowers, turnips and other vegetables. It was already known that Oscar had bitter enemies as well as a large crowd of friends. And if his chief enemy was eccentric, many of his jealous rivals were quite unscrupulous.

It was a freezing cold night, and a black bitter wind blew on Valentine's Day, the 14th February 1895, that date of the last first night.

3. Afterwards

The disagreement of the jury after the first trial left Oscar, after his agonising ordeal, free for the time. But all the hotels, clubs and even a large number of private friends who had been almost fighting with each other a few weeks, even days, ago to flatter and make much of him now refused point-blank to receive him at all. He was like a hunted stag, with no place to find refuge. He could not even take a room at an hotel.

And this was not that the hotels, clubs and private friends condemned him in any way at present. The question was in abeyance, everything entirely depending on what the result of the next trial might be. From place to place he went, refused everywhere, with extreme politeness certainly, for he might at any moment be reinstated and be the hero, martyr and lion of the day. But they would not take the risk.

I do not mean that he had not many loyal and devoted friends. But these were not in a position to offer him hospitality.

He seemed so unhappy with his family at this time that we asked him to stay with us, feeling that he would be more at ease with friends than with relatives. Before he came, we called all the servants together, parlour-maid, housemaid, cook, kitchen-maid and our old nurse, Mrs. Field, who acted as my maid. We told them who was coming, offering them a month's wages if they wished to leave at once. For the affair was now such a scandal as had rarely been known. Little else was talked of in London; the papers were full of it; America, Germany, all the Continent joined in the controversy, the foreigners saying, 'This is how you behave to your poets,' while the Americans said, 'This is how your poets behave.' Each servant in turn refused to leave. They appeared proud to wait on 'poor Mr. Wilde,' to whom indeed they had been devoted ever since he had started coming to the house. We sent the coachman away for a holiday, as we feared he might talk in public-houses. The others promised to keep the secret.

Then I went to fetch Oscar. He accepted with joy. And he came back with me in the little pill-box brougham. When we arrived I showed him his rooms, the nursery floor, which was almost a flat in itself, two big rooms, one small one, and a bathroom. My little boy was in the country at the time.

I asked him if he would like me to take away the toys in the room. " Please leave them," he said. So, in the presence of a rocking-horse, dolls' houses, golliwogs, a blue and white nursery dado with rabbits and other animals on it, the most serious and tragic matters were discussed. The poet leant his elbow on the American cloth of the nursery table, and talked over the coming trial with his solicitor.

While all our friends as well as the whole public were discussing Oscar, no one had any idea that he was under our roof.

He made certain rules in order to avoid any embarrassment for us. He never left the nursery floor till six o'clock. He had breakfast, luncheon and tea up there, and received all his loyal friends there. He never would discuss his troubles before me; such exaggerated delicacy seems to-day almost incredible. But every day at six he would come down dressed for dinner, and talk to me for a couple of hours in the drawing-room. As always he was most carefully dressed, there was a flower in his buttonhole, and he had received his usual daily visit from the old hairdresser who shaved him and waved his hair. His ambition was always to look like a Roman bust.

The old nurse, who waited on him, simply adored him. She always said "I never believe a word against Mr. Wilde. He's a gentleman, if ever there was one." Beerbohm Tree agreed with her, "He remained *grand seigneur* to the last."

When we were alone, he would walk up and down the room, always smoking a cigarette, talking in the most enchanting way about everything except his trouble.

Sometimes he would improvise prose poems, like those published in his works. Once he asked for writing things, to note down one of these improvisations. I could not find any. "You have all the equipment of a writer, my dear Sphinx, except pens, ink and paper."

One day he was talking of the effect of absinthe. "After the first glass, you see things as you wish they were. After the second, you see them as they are not. Finally you see things as they really are, and that is the most horrible thing in the world."

"How do you mean?"

"I mean disassociated. Take a top-hat! You think you see it as it really is. But you don't, because you associate it with other things and ideas. If you had never heard of one before, suddenly saw it alone, you'd be frightened, or laugh. That is the effect absinthe has, and that is why it drives men mad."

He went on. "Three nights I sat up all night drinking absinthe, and thinking that I was singularly clear-headed and sane. The waiter came in and began watering the sawdust. The most wonderful flowers, tulips, lilies and roses sprang up and made a garden of the *café*. 'Don't you see them?' I said to him. 'Mais non, Monsieur; il n'y a rien.' "

He was also very romantic about opium and other drugs. He could not take them himself, they made him prosaically ill. Oscar loved to talk of the frequenters of the opium-dens in Limehouse. 'Who knows in what strange heaven they are suffering, what dull hells are teaching them the secret of some new joy?' He was the least neurotic man imaginable, and though Baudelaire and Poe appealed enormously to his imagination, he was utterly unlike them. He so much enjoyed everything, a joke, a sunset, talking to a child, that it was unnecessary for him, one felt, to 'chercher midi à quatorze heures.'

After dinner I would leave him with his

friends; it was the only time of the day that they made serious plans, or, in fact, talked sense.

Generally he was extremely optimistic, firmly believing in a palmist's prophecy of triumph. One day his wife came to see him. They were alone for two hours.

I loved her very much, and was grieved to see her leave in tears. I found afterwards that she had come with an urgent message from her lawyer imploring him to go away without fail before the next trial which would undoubtedly be his ruin.

Then came a look of immovable obstinacy on to his face. Nothing on earth would induce him to leave, though he knew that every facility was given to him. His mother told him it would be dishonourable for him to leave. Moreover, he never expected anything in his life to turn out badly.

Frank Harris tells the story of the yacht he had been lent to do what he liked with, and which was waiting to take the poet away. One evening he came to propose this to the poet, and asked me if I could row. Of course I said 'yes,' and saw myself as a fine ferryman. But Oscar absolutely refused.

The only time I ever suggested his going, I

sent him up a little note, begging him to do as his wife asked him. When he came down to dinner, he gave me back my note, saying "That is not like you, Sphinx." And then he began to talk of books.

He never liked even the grotesque part of Dickens. To those who praised Dickens, he said 'One must have a heart of stone to read the death of Little Nell without laughing.'

Of Max Beerbohm he said, 'He plays with words as one plays with what one loves.' Adding, 'When you are alone with him, Sphinx, does he take off his face and reveal his mask?'

The morning came when he was to leave for his ordeal. The night before he had asked me to put a sleeping-draught on his mantelpiece. He never intended to take it, but just the presence of it had, he said, a magical effect.

In the hall he suddenly turned to me and said, for the first time in a faltering voice, "If the worst comes to the worst, Sphinx, you'll write to me?"

Then he and his friend, Mr. Adey, left in the little pill-box brougham which I had hired for him.

Later on the same day I received a telegram

to tell me what had happened. I did not see him again for two years.

When Oscar was again a free man, he found himself without his mother and his brother, who both had died, and without his children—for whom a guardian had been appointed. But he felt most of all the death of his wife. She came to see him very frequently during the two years; always she was kind and devoted. Then she was ill, and died at Genoa after an operation.

This was the greatest blow to Oscar. As soon as possible he went to Genoa and visited her grave. He drove out to it in a little ramshackle fly, a green one. He abandoned himself to a passion of grief, repentance and bitter remorse; and amid the lavish crimson roses with which he covered the grave, he broke down, sobbed and prayed, and made vows of eternal fidelity to her memory. He had been very sincerely in love with her, and he felt now that only some madness had made him cause her sorrow. He was shattered and broken after this violent emotion, and shed tears in the fly as he was driven away.

In his curious temperament there were many contradictions. Suddenly his sadness left him.

He became peculiarly gay and almost reckless. And it was several days before he thought to dismiss the cab.

Oscar once told a friend of a strange experience that he never forgot and later often thought of.

When first married, he was quite madly in love, and showed himself an unusually devoted husband. He never left his wife for an hour, and she adored him in return. A few months after their marriage, she went shopping, and Oscar accompanied her. He waited for her outside Swan and Edgar's while she made some long and tedious purchases.

As he stood there full of careless good spirits, on a cold sunny May morning, a curious, very young, but hard-eyed creature appeared, looked at him, gave a sort of laugh, and passed on. He felt, he said, 'as if an icy hand had clutched his heart.' He had a sudden presentiment. He saw a vision of folly, misery and ruin. And remained in a depressed state for the rest of the evening.

Very early one very cold May morning my husband, I, and several other friends drove from our house in Deanery Street to meet

Oscar at the house in Bloomsbury of the Rev. Stuart Headlam. The drawing-room was full of Burne-Jones and Rossetti pictures, Morris wallpaper and curtains, in fact an example of the decoration of the early 'eighties, very beautiful in its way, and very like the aesthetic rooms Oscar had once loved.

We all felt intensely nervous and embarrassed. We had the English fear of showing our feelings, and at the same time the human fear of not showing our feelings.

He came in, and at once he put us at our ease. He came in with the dignity of a king returning from exile. He came in talking, laughing, smoking a cigarette, with waved hair and a flower in his button-hole, and he looked markedly better, slighter, and younger than he had two years previously. His first words were, "Sphinx, how marvellous of you to know exactly the right hat to wear at seven o'clock in the morning to meet a friend who has been away! You can't have got up, you must have sat up." He talked on lightly for some time, then wrote a letter, and sent it in a cab to a Roman Catholic Retreat, asking if he might retire there for six months. While waiting, he walked up and down, and said: "The dear Governor, such a delightful man, and his wife is charming. I spent happy hours in their garden, and they asked me to spend the summer with them. They thought I was the gardener." He began to laugh. "Unusual, I think? but I don't feel I can. I feel I want a change of scene."

"Do you know one of the punishments that happen to people who have been 'away?' They are not allowed to read *The Daily Chronicle!* Coming along I begged to be allowed to read it in the train. 'No!' Then I suggested I might be allowed to read it upside down. This they consented to allow, and I read all the way *The Daily Chronicle* upside down, and never enjoyed it so much. It's really the only way to read newspapers."

The man returned with the letter. We all looked away while Oscar read it. They replied that they could not accept him in the Retreat at his impulse of the moment. It must be thought over for at least a year. In fact they refused him.

Then he broke down and sobbed bitterly. I left, and heard later that he went to Berneval with friends. Oscar had a wonderful power of recuperation, and soon recovered his spirits.

Later I went to Paris to see him, and found him at that time leading the life of a student in a tiny room at the Hotel d'Alsace. He was unique in his power of making people fond of him. It is known that his landlord lent him hundreds of pounds.

In this sketch, for it is no more, I am making no attempt to criticise or appraise either the man or his work. I speak solely of what was in my personal knowledge.

Oscar was the most generous man I have ever met, and he showed his kindness always in the most graceful way.

A young solicitor whom he knew only slightly, told him that he was madly in love with a marvellously lovely girl of sixteen. She had red hair, violet eyes, and black eyelashes, and had a great likeness to the portraits of Rossetti's wife and the wife of William Morris. Her name was Marjorie.

"How much would you actually need in order to marry Marjorie?" asked Oscar.

"A hundred and fifty pounds. Then I could take a tiny flat and work. She is earning her own living."

Oscar had just received a large sum for *Lady Windermere's Fan*. He wrote a cheque that moment for a hundred and sixty pounds, and gave it to the young man, saying peremptorily,

"Go *at once*, and marry her, boy, and bring her to our house at Worthing for your honeymoon."

He did so, and Oscar was worshipped by them both ever afterwards. Marjorie was the only other woman who went to meet him after he had been 'away.' She was quite as incredibly lovely as the young man had said, and very sweet and clever.

He had many devoted friends, who remained always loyal to him. Chief among these was Robert Ross. There was indeed no trouble he would not take to advance a friend's interest, and I think he rather resented any friend who was not in actual need of help. *A propos* of this, Oscar Wilde once improvised a fable in the style of the Lives of the Saints. He called it Saint Robert of Phillimore. (It was in Phillimore Gardens that Robbie's people lived.)

Saint Robert of Phillimore

There was a certain Saint, who was called Saint Robert of Phillimore. Every night, while the sky was yet black, he would rise from his bed and, falling on his knees, pray to God that He, of His great bounty, would cause the sun to rise and make bright the earth. And always, when the sun rose, Saint Robert knelt again and thanked God that this miracle had been vouchsafed. Now, one night, Saint Robert, wearied by the vast number of more than usually good deeds that he had done that day, slept so soundly that when he awoke the sun had already risen, and the earth was already bright. For a few moments Saint Robert looked grave and troubled, but presently he fell down on his knees and thanked God that, despite the neglectfulness of His servant, He had yet caused the sun to rise and make bright the earth.

One of the hits in *The Importance of being Earnest* is when the clergyman says that Mr. Bunbury expressed a desire to be buried in Paris. 'I fear,' says the clergyman, 'that this doesn't seem a very desirable state of mind at the last.'

Oscar is buried in Paris under Epstein's magnificent monument given, ten years after his death, by a lady* whose friendship remained steadfast to the end.

---

* It was the beautiful Mrs. Carew, the mother of Sir Coleridge Kennard. I have his permission to mention her name, which has hitherto remained secret.

Letters to the Sphinx from Oscar Wilde

1893

(TELEGRAM)

The author of the Sphinx will on Wednesday at two eat pomegranates with the Sphinx of Modern Life.

May

Dear Sphinx,

Your letter was wonderful and delightful.

The 'Minx' I long to read. It is a brilliant title. Your feast was rose-like. Quite soon I hope to meet.

OSCAR

16 Tite Street,
S.W.

Dear Sphinx,

Any night next week, except Monday, I shall be charmed to come and dine with you. Of course I sit next you.

By all means have red candleshades.

I delight in your literary 'minx'. It is most brilliant, but should be longer; we want more of it.

Yours,
OSCAR

16 Tite Street,
Chelsea, S.W.

Alas! dear Sphinx, I believe we are going to 'La Femme de Claude' to-night, otherwise I would eat honey cakes with you at Willis's.

Punch is delightful, and the drawing a masterpiece of clever caricature. I am afraid she was a minx after all! You are the only Sphinx.

Yours,
OSCAR

My dear Sphinx,

Can I see you to-night? I mean, are you disengaged or have you friends?

Yours,
OSCAR

Florence

Dear Sphinx,

This quite wrong rose-coloured paper was left here by someone else, and I am using it by mistake.

You are one of those—alas, too few—who are always followed by the flutes of the Pagan World.

Yours,
OSCAR

1893

Albemarle Club

Your sketch is brilliant, as your work always is.

It is quite tragic for me to think how completely Dorian Gray has been understood on all sides!

Why don't you collect your wonderful, witty, delightful sketches—so slight, so suggestive, so full of 'esprit' and intellectual sympathy?

You are one of those who, in art, are always, by intuition, behind the scenes—so you see how natural art is.

OSCAR WILDE

16 Tite Street,
S.W.

Dear Sphinx,

Your dialogue is brilliant and delightful and dangerous. I am quite charmed with it. What the Comtesse Gyp has done in France for Life, you have done in England for Art. No one admires your clever, witty subtle style more than I do. Nothing pains me except stupidity.

OSCAR WILDE

16 Tite Street

Might it be Wednesday or Thursday or Friday?

I am just told that there are to be feasters here on Tuesday. Do let me know. All my other days in the weeks belong to you.

How wilful and wonderful you are!

Ever yours,
OSCAR

1894

16 Tite Street,
S.W.

Dear Sphinx,

I have a *Salome* for you—when can I bring it to you?

Have you seen *The Yellow Book?* It is horrid, and not yellow at all.

Yours,
OSCAR

Hotel Metropole,
Brighton
Friday

Dear Sphinx,

I hope to be in London on the 15th, will you be there?

Your article in *Punch* I read with joy, and detected you, of course, before you sent it to me.

My friend is not allowed to go out to-day: I sit by his side and read him passages from his own life. They fill him with surprise. Everyone should keep someone else's diary; I sometimes suspect you of keeping mine.

Is your birthday really the 10th? Mine is the 16th! How tragic: I fear that looks like brother and sister. Perhaps it is better so.

Yours,

OSCAR

(TELEGRAM)

July 25th, 1894

Remember Pomegranates at Willis 8 o'c Friday.

OSCAR

Worthing
September 22nd, 1894

Esmé and Reggie* are delighted and disappointed to find that their Sphinx is not a minx after all. Reggie goes up to-night to Cadogan Place, and proposes to call on the dear and rarely treacherous Sphinx to-morrow. —The doubting disciple who has written the false gospel is one who has merely talent unrelieved by any flashes of physical beauty.

OSCAR

* Characters in *The Green Carnation*.

Worthing

Dear Sphinx,

Of course you have been deeply wronged. But there are many bits in *The Green Carnation* not unworthy of your brilliant pen; and treachery is inseparable from faith; I often betray myself with a kiss.

Robert Hichens I did not think capable of anything so clever. It is such a bore about journalists, they are so very clever!

How sweet of you to have *Intentions* bound for your birthday! I simply love that book.

I shall be in town soon and must come and charm the Sphinx with honey-cakes. The trouble is, I left my flute in a railway carriage and the Fauns take so long to cut new reeds.

Yours,
OSCAR

Am so pleased, my dear Sphinx. No other voice but yours is musical enough to echo my music. I rely on you to misrepresent me. Your article will be worthy of you and of me. Have you a box to-morrow night? If so, I will come, as I am still forbidden to go out.

OSCAR

Hotel Albemarle,
Piccadilly

Dear Sphinx,

Oh! How rash of you to trust me with your brilliant article! I had put it into a casket, and thrown the key into the waters. But now I have shattered the casket and send you the purple papyrus of your perfect panegyric—so full of instinct, of subtlety, of charm—a real model of appreciation. I hope it will be published and in an edition de luxe!

Yes, I fly to Algiers to-morrow. I begged my friend to let me stay to rehearse, but so beautiful is his nature that he declined at once.

Poste Restante,
Algiers

Do write.

Yours,
OSCAR

February 12th, 1895

Come to-night to theatre, 7.45 Dress Rehearsal without scenery. Bring Robbie or someone with you. Have secured small box for you for first night.

OSCAR

February, 1895

Dear Sphinx,   Albemarle Club

You are more than all criticisms. It only remains for me to thank you a thousand times for your desire to blow in my honour a daffodil-shaped horn.   Ever yours,

OSCAR

Bosie sends sweet words, and so does our Scotch friend, Ross.

*   *   *

Holloway

Dear Sphinx,   *9. 4. 1895*

I write to you from prison, where your kind words have reached me and given me comfort though they have made me cry, in my loneliness. Not that I am really alone. A slim thing, gold-haired, like an angel, stands always at my side, whose presence overshadows me, moving in the gloom like a white flower.

With what a crash this fell! Why did the Sibyl say fair things? I thought but to defend him from his Father; I thought of nothing else, and now—

I can't write more. How good and kind and sweet you are to me!   OSCAR

[*It must be said that the friend for whom Oscar*

evinced such an extraordinary affection had everything to interest a lover of poetry. Very handsome, he had a great look of Shelley. Not only was he an admirable athlete, he had won various cups for running at Oxford, but he had a strong sense of humour and a wit quite of his own and utterly different from Oscar's. His charm made him extremely popular, and he wrote remarkable poetry. Nor was Oscar indifferent to the romance of his ancient Scottish lineage.]

Holloway

17. 4. 1895

I hear that wonderful things are being done for me---by people of noble beautiful souls and natures.

Of course I cannot thank you. Words may not bear such burdens. I cannot even try. I merely say that you will always remain in a niche of a heart—half broken already—as a most dear image of all that in life has love and pity in it.

As for me, the wings of great love encompass me! holy ground.

With deep affection and gratitude.

Yours,

OSCAR

Holloway
23. 4. 1895

My dear Sphinx,

I have just had a charming note from you. How good you are to me!

I don't know what to do; my life seems to have gone from me, I feel caught in a terrible net. I don't know where to turn. I care less when I think of who is thinking of me, I think of nothing else.

OSCAR

Holloway
2. 5. 1896

Dear and wonderful Sphinx,

Will you send me some books? I would like some Stevensons, *The Master of Ballantrae* and *Kidnapped*. I have no one who brings me books, so I come to you, for you are so good to me that I am glad to think that I never can repay you. Life is not long enough to allow it. Always, always, I shall be in your debt.

Your letters cheered me very much. I do hope to see you soon.

I have had no letter as yet to-day from Fleur-de-lys. I wait with strange hunger for it.

My warmest thanks.

Always yours in gratitude and affection.

OSCAR

May, 1895

My dear Sphinx,

Your Shakespeare has arrived safely, and I hear your books are below. I hope I shall be allowed to have them as Sunday is such a long day here.

I had two letters from Jonquil to-day, to make up, and I saw Frank Harris. He was very pleasant and I think will be able to help me. I have just written to Calais to say how sweet you are to me. I believe I come out on Tuesday next. I must see you, of course.

Ever with great affection.

Yours,
OSCAR

Holloway
6. 5. 1895

My dear Sphinx,

I have not had a line to-day from Fleur-de-lys. I suppose he is at Rouen. I am so wretched when I don't hear, and to-day I am bored and sick of the death of this place. I am reading your books, but I want to be out, and with people I love. The days are endless.

Your kindness makes things better for me. I go on trespassing on it more and more.

Oh! I hope all will come well, and that I can go back to Art and Life! Here I sicken in inanition.

Ever with great affection.

Yours,

OSCAR

Letter from Rouen just arrived. Please wire my thanks. I am cured of sorrow for to-day.

Dear Sphinx,

I am so sorry you are ill and upset. You have been all goodness and sweet kindness to me.

I am always your grateful and devoted friend. OSCAR

(TELEGRAM)

May 8th, 1895

Am staying at 146 Oakley Street for a few days. Can I call this evening?

OSCAR

My dear sweet kind Friend,

I have no words to thank you for all you do for me—but for you I have deepest love.

I hope to be in better spirits to-night.

Your sweetness last night was wonderful. Your flowers are like him, and your sending

them like yourself. Dear, dear friend—to-night I see you at 7.45. Ah! you are good and gentle and wonderful always.   Devotedly
                                    Yours,
                                       OSCAR

My dear Sphinx,

Thank you again and again, but I fear I can make no definite promise about to-morrow, as I am not well to-day. I have nervous prostration, so perhaps I had better do nothing till my Sunday evening with you. To that I look forward, I need hardly say—with all deep feeling towards you.

I heard to-day from Rouen.

No more at present as I am ill.

Your affectionate and devoted Friend.
                                       OSCAR

After Two Years

                    Hotel Sandwich,
                         Dieppe
Dear Sphinx,   *1897*

I was so charmed with seeing you yesterday morning that I must write a line to tell you how sweet and good it was of you to be the very first to greet me. When I think that Sphinxes are minions of the moon, and that you got up early before dawn, I am filled with wonder and joy.

I often thought of you in the long black days and nights of my sad life, and to find you just as wonderful and dear as ever was no surprise; the beautiful are always beautiful.

It is my first day of real liberty, so I try to send you a line.

Ever affectionately yours,

OSCAR WILDE

I am stopping here as Sebastian Melmoth—not Esqre, but Monsieur Sebastian Melmoth.

Reggie Turner is staying here under the name 'Robert Ross,' Robbie under the name 'Reginald Turner.' It is better they should not use their own names.

Hotel de la Plage,
Berneval-sur-Mer,
Dieppe

My dear Sphinx, *May, 1897*

Thanks for your charming letter.

I knew about the rape of the Duchess of Padua; it is, of course, a ten-act tragedy now: the last five acts in prose. I know you are just as sorry as I am. We simply must be sorry together. I still hope she is only hiding in some carved chest, or behind green-blue tapestries on which hunters blow silent horns. You have a lovely voice; so perhaps if you called to her three times she would come out. If so, pray call four times.

The date of your letter is only 'June': a date quite accurate enough when a golden rose is writing.

When, however, the golden rose, instead of merely chronicling her own petals, insists on stating there is a notice of your letter in *The Daily Chronicle* of *to-day* and asks me "Have I seen it?" I am troubled. If you can remember what day it was, would you let me see the notice? I am in the Public Press sometimes the 'ex-convict' which is too obvious; and sometimes '*le poète forçat*,' which I like, as it puts me into good company; sometimes I am 'Mr Oscar Wilde,' a phrase I remember; sometimes 'the man Wilde,' a phrase I don't. So I like to know how I am spoken of. To be spoken of, and not to be spoken to, is delightful.

I would love to see you, I need hardly say.

To-day is hot heart of summer: but all the wind is in the trees: the sea is a burning-glass.

Ever affectionately yours,

OSCAR

www.ingramcontent.com/pod-product-compliance
Ingram Content Group UK Ltd.
Pitfield, Milton Keynes, MK11 3LW, UK
UKHW011051080825
461628UK00006BA/52